THE PORTAGE POETRY SERIES

I0559739

SERIES TITLES

PRAISE FOR

tic tic tic

"One can only applaud Heidi Seaborn's spiritual and intellectual acumen. More than testimonial, the poems in *tic tic tic* bring to our age of volatility and urgent moral questions, a clear-sightedness owed to her Eliotic sense of history and rich literary knowledge. *tic tic tic* gently and magically reorients our eyes, turns us toward the light of awareness where language is action."

—MAJOR JACKSON
author of *Razzle Dazzle*

"There is clock time and there is human time. 'Any timepiece can be set right again—but the pace clicks up a notch,' writes Heidi Seaborn, and she beautifully, movingly tracks and enacts an accelerating motion of insight through the inner and outer seasons of these challenging times."

—ARTHUR SZE
author *of Into the Hush*

"The poems of *tic tic tic* are part meditative metronome and part photographic timeline documenting what it's been like to love, have children, have grandchildren, travel, and be alive as the daily news delivers unending reports of death, sorrow, and despair. Decade after decade "in the millennium crawling across the continuum," time does not give one time to pause for the shock of yet another king's atrocities. Heidi Seaborn's poems foreground moments of resonance: the clicking of a camera capturing a sunset in 1984 is also "[t]icking / across time," spider season yields a patient spider, and a daughter reaches to her dead father from the now. These poems syncopate—rising like the wild heartbeats of those who hope."

—DIANA KHOI NGUYEN
author of *Root Fractures*

"*tic tic tic* reminds me that poems, with their surprising observations and cadences, can create small but vital openings in the armor of our protective gestures, portals through which thought and feeling move, mind to mind and heart to heart; they create conditions of vulnerability and leave their records of motion, even when subjects appear still. The spiraled nature of time as experienced by a human consciousness, in Seaborn's evocation here, is not a dizzying spin so much as a steady, private documentation of places where quietude and tumult converge: a precisely arranged accumulation of turning vantages, details, and quotations. Orbiting dynamic questions of faith, grief, and time, these vivid poems grapple with ongoingness and unfinishedness: 'The end of the day—will not / end its spiral / descent to / another place—' Seaborn writes, 'call it a life or a death.'"

—GABRIELLE BATES
author of *Judas Goat*

tic tic tic

poems

Heidi
Seaborn

CORNERSTONE PRESS
UNIVERSITY OF WISCONSIN-STEVENS POINT

Cornerstone Press, Stevens Point, Wisconsin 54481
Copyright © 2025 Heidi Seaborn
www.uwsp.edu/cornerstone

Printed in the United States of America.

Library of Congress Control Number: 2025941760
ISBN: 978-1-968148-07-2

All rights reserved.

Cover Art: "Passing Through Time" at the Musee d'Orsay in Paris © Eric Falk

Interior Art:
"Cable Crucifixes" © Jack Sinclair
"Burned trees on a winter's day" © Keith Skelton
"Fear/Hope" © Jack Sinclair
"Bird on barbed wire" © Esther Moliné (esthermolinephotograph.com)
"Violinist in Concert" © suteishi
"Possibility" ©Jack Sinclair
"Lying Among Giants" © Jack Sinclair
"Addiction" © feri ferdinan
"Class Photo" public domain
"Ultrasound, Fetal Foot" public domain
"Airplane in the Sky" public domain
From "Snow covered farm in central Virginia" series © Montes-Bradley
"A Day Gone By" © Jack Sinclair
"Wildfire" public domain
"Jellyfish" © Keith Skelton
"Hat Chao Mai" © Utopia_88
"Amusing Ourselves to Death" © Jack Sinclair
"Heart Murmur" © Maggie Henfield
"Blue Sky" public domain
"Bird Tree" © James Crombie

Cornerstone Press titles are produced in courses and internships offered by the
Department of English at the University of Wisconsin–Stevens Point.

DIRECTOR & PUBLISHER   EXECUTIVE EDITORS
Dr. Ross K. Tangedal   Jeff Snowbarger, Freesia McKee

EDITORIAL DIRECTOR   SENIOR EDITORS
Brett Hill   Paige Biever, Eva Nielsen, Reilly Crous

PRESS STAFF
Lilly Kulbeck, Josh Paulson, Sophie McPherson, Sam Bjork, Madison Schultz, Autumn Vine, Allison Lange

For my children and their children

ALSO BY HEIDI SEABORN:

Books
Marilyn: Essays & Poems
An Insomniac's Slumber Party with Marilyn Monroe
Give a Girl Chaos {see what she can do}

Chapbooks
Bite Marks
Once a Diva
Finding My Way Home

CONTENTS

I. WINTER

II. SPRING

III. SUMMER

IV. AUTUMN

i pray for time
to deal with now. no, i pray to *Time.*
—Danez Smith

I.

Winter

We are living through a time
that needs to be lived through us
—Adrienne Rich

Adieu, farewell, earth's bliss;
This world uncertain is;

—Thomas Nashe

ACCIDIE

I have lived a thousand days
like today the sluggish sky

dragging a finger through clouds.
So much silence—

each yellow door closing.
The bowl of fruit carefully

arranged so the apples don't spoil
the bananas.

Clean dishrags creased
along the oven door

like white teeth.
I am no longer hungry.

Am overfed. Have fed the orchids
ice. When I shift away

from the sun, my faith cools.
If I stay here long enough. If I long
enough.

TIME CAPSULE

Eye Mask, 2019

Such luxury to discover sloth in my cash-
mere years. As if I had only now woken
into sunlight slanting through blinds. The
afternoon's tea spilling over the newspa-
per, muting all those cries for help.

CONTINUUM

for the many dead
in *this residence of woe*—
And me, holding a family wedding photo.

*

1 January 2020

When the weather turned anxious—
the bright cheek of autumn grayed.

In a chartreuse-lit lab—
In a gold-strafed bureau—
men construe a new world—

The lifted bow of another year hovers over the strings—
the season freezes in a glass of bourbon

I drink as the balloons fall and the burlesque queen sings—
Auld lang syne my friends!

And we kiss another decade in the millennium crawling across the continuum—
Then—

Winter/Spring 2020

Wo warst du wann? I was skiing, old limbs to tree runs—
bracing the Wyoming cold. Hadn't I seen a moose—
loose beneath the lift? Such good luck. À votre *santé!*
A sniffle and a line dance in the cowboy bar at night.

Forgive me, my love, we were silly. the clock tower warning—
wringing its snow-covered hands. So cold. So cold—
a white kimono fastening over our hearts,
the blue-lipped kiss of the *yuki- onna* on wintered earth.

I slept in that month and the next until the mackerel
dragged the sea lions inland. Until the lilacs flurried.
I'd forgotten to rush out the door. Forgotten the crush—

As if the fortune teller had thrown the Major Arcana card—
As if the white horse had thrown the skeleton—
So much change in my pocket and no one takes it anymore—

We all know someone, we said. You or you or the other.
Immune sounds like commune but it's not the same.

I had not thought death had undone so many wrote Eliot. On a walk—
the parade I join twice daily, faces cloistered—
bright eyes, bright eyes. *Following the river of death downstream.*

I wave to Rick, the bookseller. To Claudia, another poet.
My words churned beneath the lane of cars
cruising Beach Drive there is no-
where to go and everywhere.

I spade my garden after the hyacinths
die. Drop in seeds that promise bees and butterflies—
The carcass of winter turned over while I was sleeping—
revealing a portal.

Who would we greet there in our pajamas
while PBS gives nightly tribute to the dead? We mourn
through a box at a box. Grief squared—
What are my odds? Singing *Che ci toglie il respire*
from my balcony.

In the heat of the moment, I think to escape prayer, not
my thing. Yet, as the months engrave their weary hours—
as thousands became millions become you and you and others—
as the world turns inward, like a lazy eye—
and then ruptures, my meditations become laments—
then petitions. My piety, my hypocrisy.

Winter 2020-21

Haven't I blacked out often? Forgotten—
where I am. Where am I?
The bars remain half empty, masked in—
gloom from much too much. They say variant, virus—
I hear Vivaldi's *L'Inverno allegro non molto.*

A year of tangled bedsheets, the bathrobe of evening.
Windows clicking on and off with a frozen handwave—
Goodbye! We've stopped counting, math skills slipping
across the ice. It is winter solstice, dark at dawn

and the *barbarous king* lies in his gold-encrusted chambers, *a burnished throne*—
Drawn velvet drapes scrape the carpets where the minions kneel
playing a game of checkers. Plotting the king's leap backwards—
over the uncrowned masses. But what do I know?

I worry the dishrag, purge the cupboards, guillotine onions
into stew because there's still Christmas to stage—
Bring me flesh and bring me wine. Bring me pine logs hither.
We muddle our cocktails, muddle through— a toast *probst!*
to having survived and to all who—

Listen! The first violin racing in Vivaldi's final *I'Inverno allegro*—
the pace quickening. *Yes, something's wrong. That restless*—
As the king rises from his shadows, dragging
his string puppets, his mimicry of family, his rabble—

Darkness and devils! Saddle my horses, call my train together!
And then—the Bastille stormed by the king's own men.

Nicky calls from London. *What's happening at the Capitol?*—
What to say to my son? Words elbow down the hallway of my throat—
my brain's been stungunned, and there's no ceasing the heart's
hammer, the hurrying up of CNN—
the scurrying up and over the barricades.

Live cut across the cold steps—
to run, stamping one's feet at each moment—
the high stepping crowd, the threatening clouds—
seep through the blue of my library walls.

The king whisked away in his black armored car—
Do I remember? *Do you remember— Nothing?*—
Amnesia buttons itself like a three-piece suit,
wanders the marble halls looking for the broom closet.
What have I forgotten? I can't find my keys
to the kingdom. A wall rises—

I raise my vax card to your King of Spades.
What are the odds we survive this game?

And then it's suddenly over, swept under—
as we vagabond into hope—
along the banks of the frozen Potomac.

Winter 2022

Who could forget the buttercup poet on the Capitol steps?
I thought of daffodils defying lock down—
of tulips and narcissi. Of this past year of maybe—

its dark bulb promising.
Yet today the snow persists, and cold—
war mutters in my ear.

Let's go backwards when forward fails.
Within the barricades, the violin still plays.
I hear a branch rattling at the window—

I hear battling, feel my adrenaline kick.
And I'm holding my grandbaby, her eyes
searching for light, the tendril of my voice.

And my heart's landscape lies—
under siege—glass shards, stolen relics—
And *this* world as a newborn gift—*уeü cöim.*

Who plucks the strings? Who pulls
the strings? *Some will say none of this ever happened...we were
happy and went to see the puppet shows in the park.*

As I watch my grandchild growing into the days—
somewhere in trenches, a tune summons—
a coal tit—its song, a formal offering to the icy air.

At the pulpit we weep yellow fields of flowers—
and orphans arrive at our airport to bouquets
of balloons.

Summer/Fall 2022

They asked politely but it was raining—
so I didn't stop—
for the Planned Parenthood people.
Anyway, I'm on their list.
Still the next day I thought less—

of myself, you know. Thought maybe
they need money
to ferry women out of Idaho.

Every time I think, I mean I can't not remember—
my own—
eons ago. Honestly, I'd forgotten—
until having it taken stirred memory—
And Idaho! I mean I've had sex in Idaho!

Now, as if another century, as if chattel,
as if cattle lowing in a locked barn. Good night Bess!
Good night Lulu! Good night Mabel!

Over coffee, Linda recalls Mexico—
how the border patrol looked her
over. ¿*Dónde esta?* ¿*Dónde esta?*
the coiling streets—
a grated door, the swinging
noose of a light bulb—
shithole in the floor and sheets
like a Francis Bacon painting.

O ugly uterus, they deem not really part of us—
estranged innards, impolite company—
too rude to include in any legalese—
Dis-ease with our kind, *minds full of—*
fluff. And so just like that, puff!

and now it's *as if—*
my mind and body isn't my own—
owned by the state of Idaho.

I think of my granddaughter living in a state
where a woman's body is tethered
to a stake. Sometimes a river defines—
a border and all the residue

eventually flushes—
out to sea. Other times
there's no geographic order,
just a cattle trail crossing a state line—

7 October 2023

My son's wedding—
vows beneath a California oak, vineyards marching
the hills, a fiery sunset.

I missed the news
of the cross-border attack—
I was dancing

someone hoisted a chair—
even as elsewhere, another morning was waking—
to carnage

to the reincarnation of—
the past is rotting in the future—
in this puzzle of land.

A land I thought I knew—
Knew only dust escaping a beaten rug,
a kerosene flame—

attar and sage wafting off tea the Bedouin
offered me for my endometrial pain—
I have risked so little.

Spring 2024—

The exiled king returns from the ruff—
up to his belly in muck, stench
perfumed with
        Something's always wrong. Again. Again. Again.
And aren't we too sated for seconds?

I bring my knives to the butcher for sharpening—
I tenderize the lamb leg myself—
Easter's early this year. We had thought Florida—
gawkers at the gates—*Lasciate ogne speranza, voi ch'intrate.*

I feel that sense of *déja vu*
as dictators shoulder around a game of Risk—
but there are too many to play—
and more on the way—stand by. *Bereitstehen!*

While you and I and the others hum along
to a Pearl Jam song, *Then put your seatbelt on—*
Buckle up Buckle up Buckle up!

Or is it that other tune, *Your time will come.*
the king's favorite, played with a whistle
the hounds respond to.

Way back when, I hadn't thought—
hadn't a thought. My life laid out
like a tennis court or the lanes at the bottom
of a pool. *Do you remember?*—

There was always birdsong then—
and spring and summer and autumn and winter.
Do you remember?—

Nothing—I remember the amnesia from a fall—
memory returning like a ferry in the fog.
Haven't we met before? Somewhere—

on the infinite loop, looking for a terminating
condition, an end to it all—

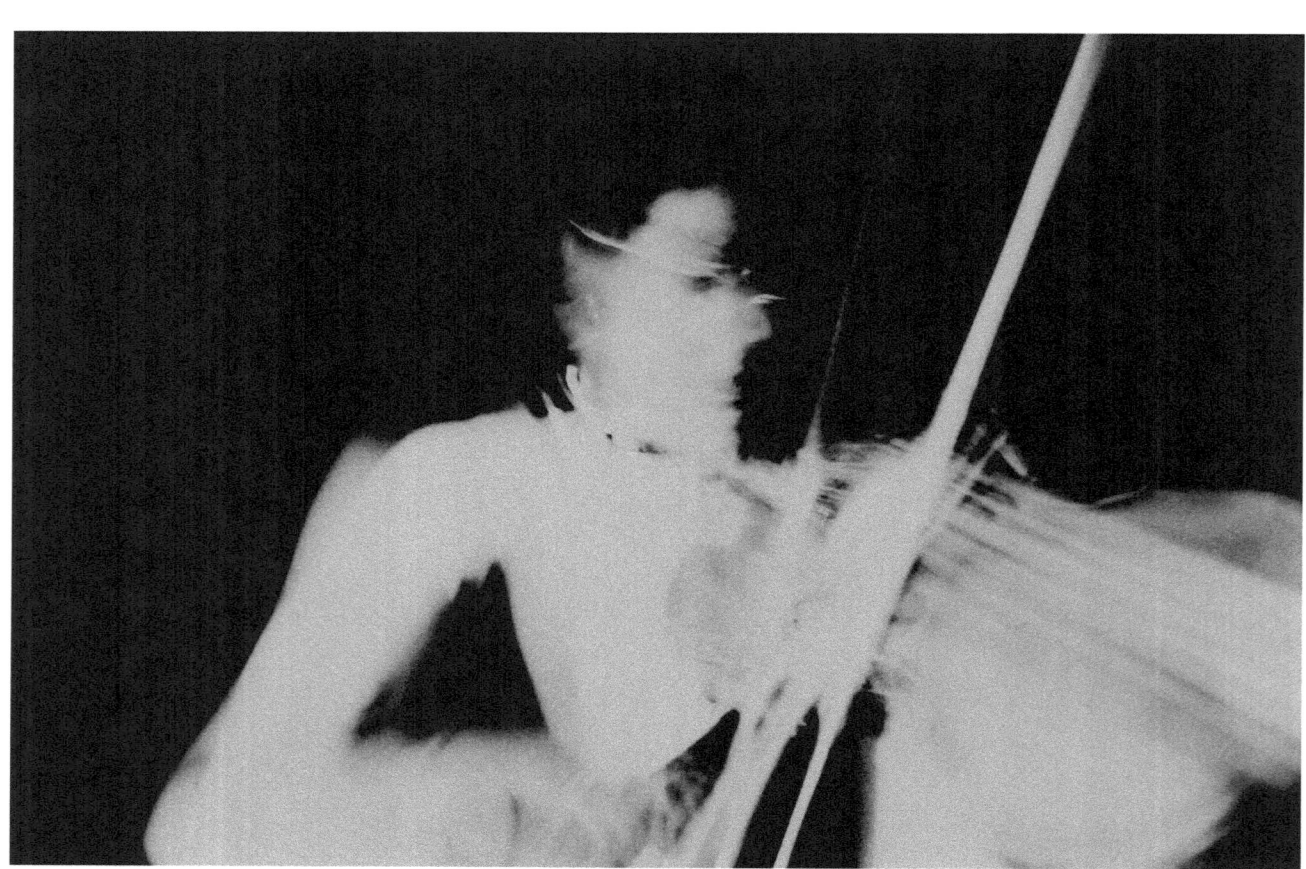

On the Continuum

On the train to D.C., to Düsseldorf, to Istanbul, to Mumbai—
          Where are we now?
          The moment you know
          You know, you know

On the hottest day ever, I enter the Sainte-Chapelle nave.
Vivaldi rising in the thickened air.
I sweat through the seasons—

Through the crescendo of tanks grinding villages to resin,
of boots on the march, again—

Doesn't it seem like every day the world burns to the ground—
as we silence the alarm—

So certain: somehow
tomorrow—
persistent as fireweed—

II.

Spring

Time collapses between the lips of strangers...
—Audre Lorde

Here from this century can you say
was it wild to be born?

Was there anything else like this, anything at all?
—Brenda Hillman

FISH STORY

This story starts with a squall
of gulls, heavy fog,
bishop pines windswept,
the Pacific somewhere
in the distance,
salmon churning
toward the Russian River.
I sit on the deck outside a cabin,
beneath a weight
of quilts. It's cold.

In the kitchen freezer,
there's a whole salmon
that I caught last summer
in a rushing river.
Gutted, then iced.
I'll eat it one day—the salmon
or is it a trout?
Whatever, it was a good weight
(twenty lbs and now it's frozen.

As I write this, I keep revising up
the weight of the fish—
the salmon or trout—
next it'll be thirty lbs.
I could go higher,
a real whopper!

Because the story about the fish—it's
a diversion.
But the squall,
the gulls, the blanketing fog,
the weight of my body—
is all true.

Well, almost.
Beneath that heaviness
of the quilts, the fog, the day—
my body was lighter,
emptied.

I'm trying to tell you: that day,
I was gutted.

IN SEARCH OF EDEN WITH KUSAMA AT
THE NEW YORK BOTANTICAL GARDEN

There's a Kusama sculpture exhibit. Gigantic blooming cartoons born of urethane and aluminum rising amongst the lilies, asters, wild rose, and black-eyed Susan's. Already the hydrangea has ceded. Only the massive pond lilies hold their own.

In the leaflet, I read of Kusama's love of nature. Think of Aristotle declaring art as imitation of nature, think of artifice.

In the native plant section, my friend Dominic introduces me to the flora and foliage by name. I follow his eye like a monarch butterfly skimming the goldenrod.

Before the Garden's conservation vault of seeds and species, I conjure Darwin aboard the HMS Beagle lolling in an undulating sea. The hull holding boxes of labeled insects, flowers, mollusks and there, the prize Galapagos finches. Wings trimmed, beaks up, tailfeathers like folded fans.

My mother traveled to the Galapagos. What did she gather there? Possibly only memories detailed in tidy hand-written diaries I'll come across one day.

As children, we knocked on doors for Earth Day, recycling drives, to scuttle development. My mother planted trees, saved a woody ravine from the bulldozer.

I bulldoze my way through the Botanical Garden, collecting photos and the surreptitious touch of leaf belly and petal. I surrender to goldfinch hovering over echinacea thistles, to the waltz of white satin moths, to the dew-bent leaves of grass, surrender to the dew, evidence nature weeps while we sleep.

Beneath an old growth forest canopy, the sky collapses into pinholes of light, imitating night.

Mark Doty, describing Eden in a poem, writes that there was *no time then but a single day.*

I long to stretch the body of this day in a hammock but the Garden is closing, returning me to the Bronx, hustling its edges like a hedge trimmer.

TIME CAPSULE

Tax Return, 1958

Sepia evidence of being 23 and father
to me. Numbers rounding into formula,
cribbed into boxes. We lived in a former
chicken coop. In my closet nursery, I
woke up to parents sunny as an egg yolk.

Photo with My Sisters, 1967

A wet comb presses our hair. We ride off
in saddle shoes. If one, if all. In the woods
behind our home, a trail disappears in
thicket. We follow until the cedars en-
circle us with their velvet arms, an owl.

Class Photo, 1969

Always in the back row with the boys
and Patty P. I can easily see all our lives
like rivers flowing onward as we lean
near the cliff of adulthood. I had only an-
swers. Questions arrived later like bees.

Map of United States, 1973

That summer, Mom drove our Ford van
cross country, ignoring her riot of kids
in the back seats. Her eyes on the prize
of NYC while I navigated the foreign
landscape, my body's new shape.

Diploma, 1980

Can a mind be documented? Spot-lit by
a gooseneck lamp bent to brighten my
brain's labors? Sharp- tooled and schooled,
the slippery cerebrum riding side saddle
into the arena. A blue-ribbon show.

Group Photo, Company Retreat 1986

After the meeting, after the boss
brushed my breast, airbrushed my con-
tribution, my being in the picture. After
words throated. After I quit. After I quit
again. After I worked my way. My way.

Stiletto, 1986

Once a man marveled at my pace. The
race I made to catch a flight. *Sprinters run
on tiptoe* I replied. Once I slipped off a red
stiletto for a man to fill with champagne.
For another, I kicked my shoes off.

Empty Pack of Marlboro Reds, 1988

And on the third try, I married a pack
of cigarettes, the cool cat at the bar. A
mouth of cinder for Cinderella. I'd been
too good a girl—it was time to take a fall,
to be dragged into the ashes of him.

Ultrasounds, 1988, 1990, 1994

Each one bloomed inside of me: a photograph developing in a dark room. And then outside me, hanging to dry, as contrasts deepened. Our eyes adjusting in the scarlet light. Focus then foci.

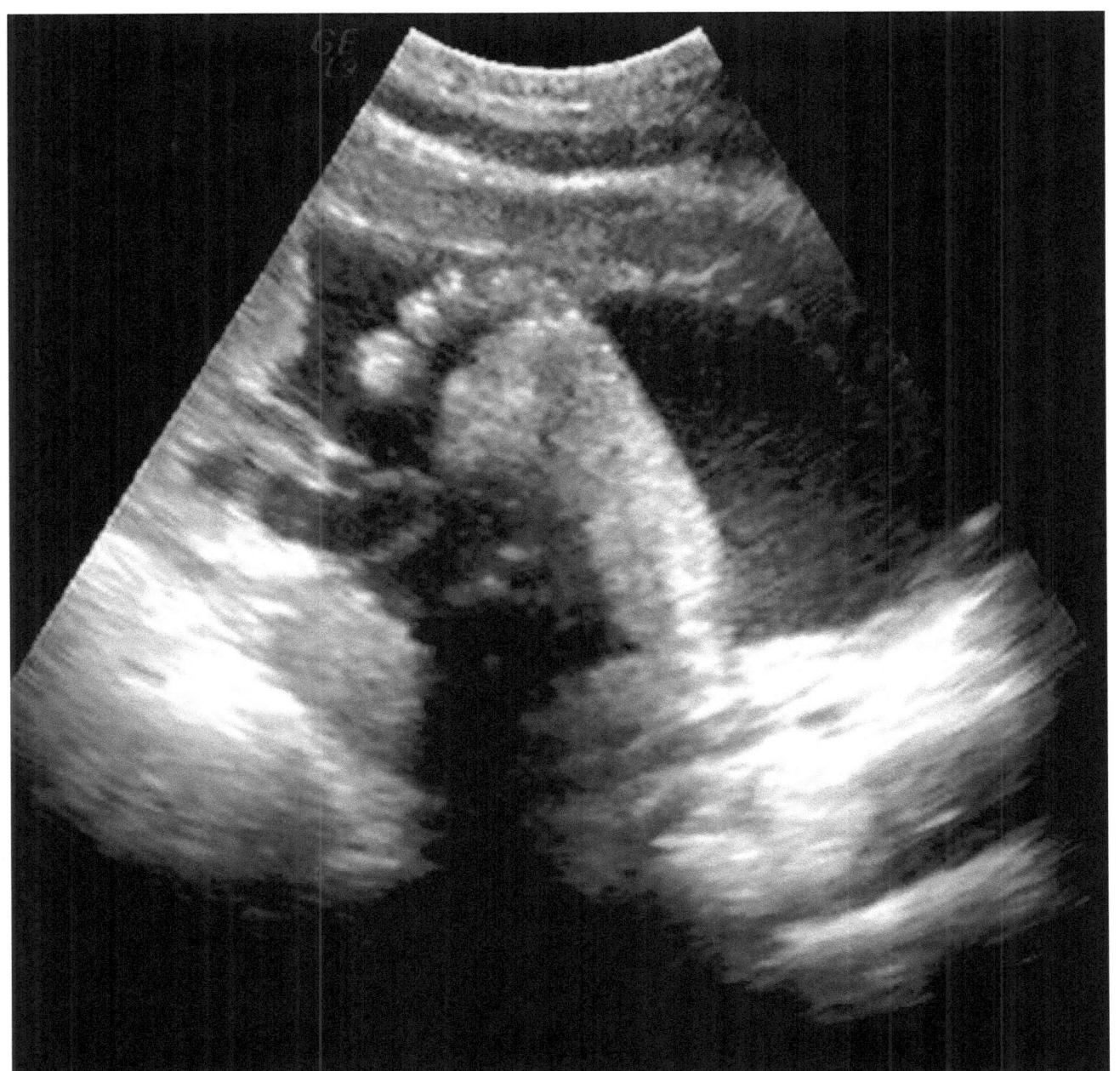

Dissected Frog, 1965-75, 1990s

As a child—a pond of polliwogs
pooled into a jar. Then in my puberty,
a pinned specimen. I crouched with
my children amongst the dragonflies
at dusk. All night, the frogs complain.

Wooden Blocks, 1990-2002

My children build a staircase that top-
ples into a valley that rivers into a sea
that crests over a land that mounds into
a mountain range that wanders into a
desert that dusts over a city of blocks.

Wall Street Journal, 2001

When the planes flew through blue and
blew the fencing I had staked around my
children as if a truck had bombed its way
down the street and on to our front lawn.
Its carcass rusting into a monument.

Passport, 1981–

Transitory tells a story of motion. Of arrivals and departures. I have seen a world rotating too quickly as if its axis was a spinning axel. Vistas of steeples and lost people as I stamp across geographies.

Paint the Town Red Nail Polish, 2010-

A little lacquer, a little late in life: when distraction is a form of attraction. *Plump Plum, Three-alarm Fire, Baby Girl Pink, Kiss Me Scarlet.* A two-dollar trip to being that woman—free of worry. Of work.

Ambien, 2001–

When my brain zips, rips, shreds the
blinking hours into ribbons. When my
body cradles a bomb within its rib cage,
I cut and lick a manufactured dream; risk
every thought I've had, and this memory.

Water Bottle, 2006–

An Aquarian, I have borne water on my hip, my head, and in the hollows of my heart. Thirst percolates in my belly. Yet only saltwater laps over my lips. The tide recedes with my fertility.

iPhone, 2009–

Window opening away from the soul.
Birds on a line, pecking one another's
feathers. Abundantly, I text ♥s and share
data like saliva. Your voice soft in my pil-
low as if we are one, breathing together.

Used Lube Tube, 2009

In a post-menopausal moment, I blush
orgasm. It is always April. Pink and
delicate. The border between desire and
lust is a pin-prick, a feather along the
spine. Mine unfurls like a moonflower.

Wedding Ring, 2011–

So often I've fallen into the myth of bliss.
Marriage begins as a semi-circle. A ring
rubs the back of aspiration. A diamond
is made from immense heat and pres-
sure. Mined in the dark, mine burns.

Obit, 2012

Grief arrives in a yellow taxi on a rainy
street corner in Manhattan. Soaked and
shivering in the back seat as it snails the
snarl. Maybe there is no destination. The
metronome of wipers, endless rain.

Face Mask, 2020

Whether crow caught in the kitchen thrashing for sky or goldfinch bashing against the brutal glass, I wing open the windows. Watch bird flight, the season change from my glass cage.

Family Wedding Photo, 2023

Proof I'd made humans who could
love, who could make other humans
from love. Our sunlit bodies (for once
no one's eyes closed) poised like wings
open for flight on the bright bird of me.

Photos of Sunsets, 1984–

The evening ritual of day dying captured
with a click. Ticking across time. Lem-
on and mandarin peel, violet, rose and,
in late summer, imperial red crashing
the horizon as the world catches fire.

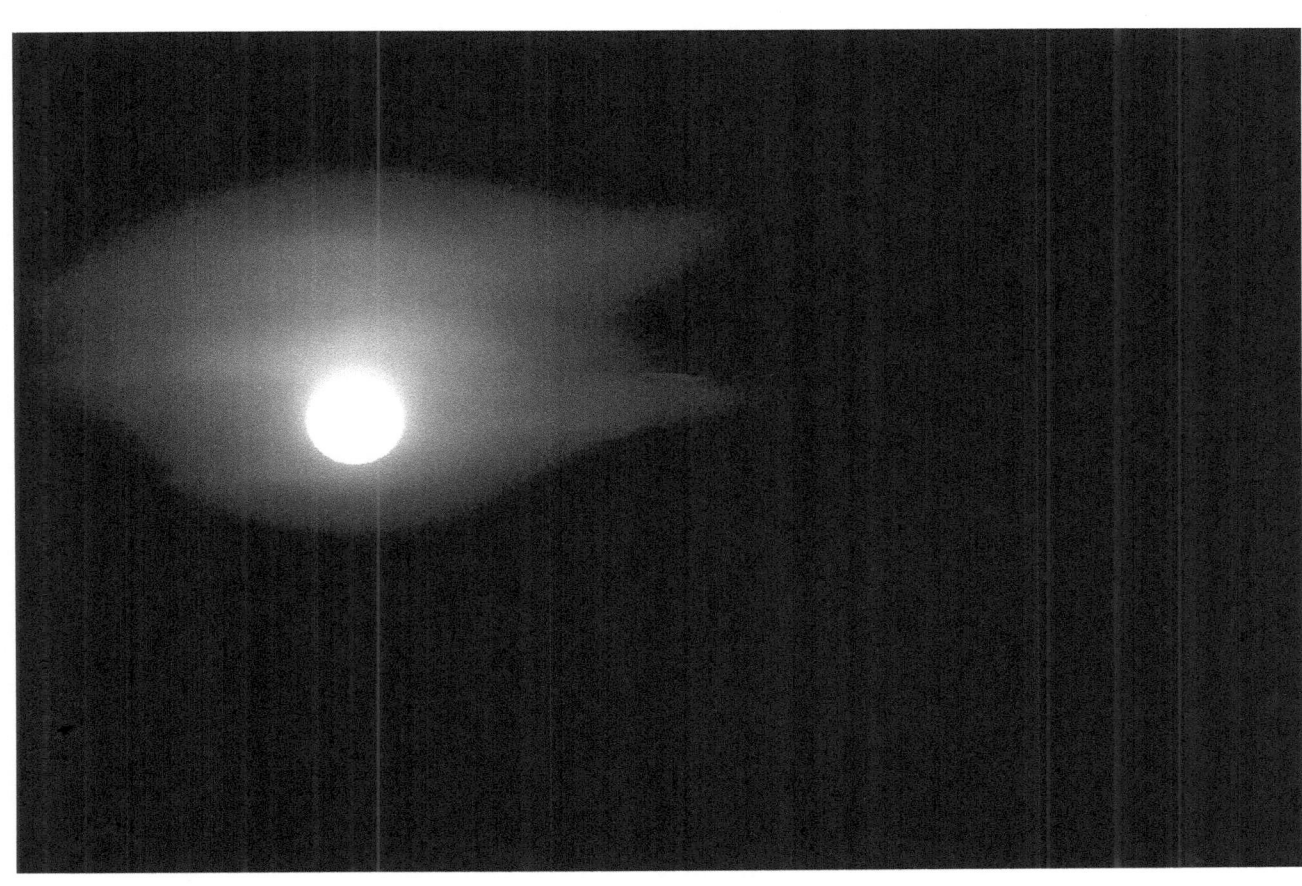

III.

Summer

I do not know which god sent me,
To fall into the river
And fall in the fire.
　　　　　—Kofi Awoonor

I know you are reading this poem, torn
between bitterness and hope.
　　　　　—Adrienne Rich

ON THE CONTINUUM

And then another summer simmers into view—
a sanguine mirage
cloaking the choke of news.

Or perhaps another season
of programming to binge, to keep my mind
from becoming a hummingbird

caught in the throat of a hawk.
I plant mahonia for the bees,
for nectar, something sweet to cut

the lingering sour aftertaste.
I walk until lost in the woods—
In a clearing, I see my error

in a shower of light—
this is the way faith asserts itself—
in a cedar cloister, in a circling ferment,

in the plague of rage. *Presto!*
e de mosche, e mosconi il Stuol furioso!
I kneel in the wrath.

LOOKOUT

1   Skagit Valley

Just before Marysville along the eastern shoulder of I-5—
a rusted dying-leaf landscape from a brush fire—
I am listening to a poet talk about refining fires—
the way Eliot thought about them—
purifying cauldron, the torching of our dross, all those sins—
It's been the hottest summer on earth—
a warehouse, Harley dealership, a 24-Hour Fitness are untouched by the fire—
This I think as I drive north, the poet's stern voice on the radio—
her poems burning like a smoke signal, and no one listens—
not even me, really. My mind meanders. A protective gesture—
It feels like the first day of fall, a crisp edge at dawn and dusk—
I am tired of brightly lit days. Weary from the harvest of grim statistics—
Here the road penetrates corn fields before winding through forest—
And what you thought you came for/is only a shell, a husk of meaning wrote Eliot—
This end that is not the end. To keep driving—
the drone of poetry keeping me from being alone—
It's been seven years since I hiked to the fire lookout near Twisp—
Seven fire seasons. I imagined living out a summer—
watching over the rippling North Cascades, watching—
the sediment of light, the sky pressing against the land, *watching whence the smoke arose*—
In Twisp, there's a small museum dedicated to smoke jumpers—
ash on an old man's sleeve. From my house, I watch the Olympics for signs—
a horizon muddled by day, ablaze at dusk. This morning there was fog—
lifting off the tousled bed of earth. Where am I driving to—
what am I driving from? *You came to kneel.* To believe—
feverish with it. And there, amongst the blur of forest, a fiery red maple—
I pull over. Cut the engine. Fall onto the maple's knuckled roots—

It is spider season. Morning sun strums web filaments—
the spider waits at its center. What is worthy of such patience—
my speed dial hunger satiated. The poet speaks of attention and brevity—
of curtailed language. Some days I hear only the loop of my own voice—
caught in the throat of a long day. Where is the bird to urge me on—
The garden stilled between summer and fall. Just the fern, and leaves—
clutching red delphinium branches. *Caught in the form of limitation*—
I look out into the silence. I look out from the silence—
The news this morning as yesterday as tomorrow—
Isn't this what Eliot meant—
when he wrote *not here the darkness in this twittering world?*—
So, I go into the garden, limber beneath the web—
its wolf spider undisturbed. Yet a crow angers the bush. I will pull out the dying—
rake the raised beds. Listening to a podcast with another poet—
the hours composting—

On the move again, this time by paddle, *the sea is all about us*—
I had hoped to go earlier, before the afternoon breezes trouble—
its surface. What will I take from this journey?—
A line of scarlet anemones, the knowledge of octopus. How short life is—
I know that's not the conclusion Eliot crusades—
From the sea, my life on land looks tender and small—
In Chinese paintings, humans appear as mites in a natural landscape—
the "I" uncentered. This year, the jellyfish are numerous—
a bloom of jellyfish, a smack of jellyfish—
In the *Compendium of Collective Nouns*, there is no term for humans—
though a multiplying of husbands might do the trick—
Abundance recenters the "I", ayes, eyes, I,I,I,I,I,I,I, ayyyyy—
So ravenous our species. Speeding until the end—
In the forest, I worship the first tree to turn toward death, *the tolling bell*—
Here on the sea, I venerate the living. *You came to kneel*—
before a turmoil of porpoises, before—

After the sea temperatures rise over 100 degrees Fahrenheit—
After the key deer, goliath grouper, sea turtles, staghorn and elkhorn coral—
this I hear on the radio driving home from the Thrift Way—
Does absence consume space? Grief swells and interrupts—
late roses filled with early snow. My mother tells me about a time shop—
clocks, watches, any timepiece can be set right again—
But the pace clicks up a notch, I feel the world panting—
as *another day/prepares for heat and silence.* And what's there—
at the end that is not the end? The billionaires ready their spacecraft—
There are only so many exits. When Maui incinerated, when—
the Atlas Mountains quaked, when the thrust of hurricane Idalia, when rivers rose—
over Emilia-Romagna, Libya, Hong Kong, *and creatures of the summer heat*—
And I can't outrun the news. It hardens into the landscape—
like volcanic magma surfacing into oxygen. Is anyone listening to the frenzy—
of poets except other poets? Did I mention the lookout near Twisp —
was long abandoned. And how every season—a wildfire. What good does it do to kneel—
before *that destructive fire?* To write the sins as if wringing the oil from a rag—
before flicking the flame? Am I not praying—
for a beginning while flecked with ashes from the end?

U̶N̶ENDING

All morning the brown birds in the tree   noise & bother over a nest. When I find
                                        the folded form of dirt
                                        brown bird on the drive
                                        later   I reach
                                        for morning as if
                                        it were a line thrown
                                        from a dock
                                        but I am drifting—
the bird chirp snagged in the wind of ticking hours. The end of the day—will not
                                        end its spiral
                                        descent to
                                        another place—
                                        call it a life or a death.
                                        Doors sway
                                        curtains ripple
                                        over a window that
bends towards an unending place of worship—the sky in all its plentitude. Here.
                                        I bear
                                        a bowl of apricots
                                        the color of sun.
                                        Can't remember when
                                        I last spoke to You—
                                        heard the wind
                                        chime of You. I mourn
each hour as if it's a bird buried beneath the blooming blue hydrangea. Grave-
                                        ness. Yet the absence
                                        of darkness.
                                        A line of crows
                                        watch over
                                        the unending
                                        glow as I grow
                                        weary

in the sun's mirror. If I could believe You—in You—I would

                                        walk the long hollow
                                        listen for wings
                                        blindly I would.
                                        Rather than lie
                                        in a poppied meadow
                                        undone by the sun—
                                        & by desire

working its claws. Yet a nest's   tender yield naked & blind waiting to wing

                                        away before branches
                                        bristle then blacken wither.
                                        Weather
                                        wanders past
                                        disguised
                                        as a friend—
                                        as You.

Each extreme cawing from somewhere near   neighbors now

                                        the blackbirds
                                        clamor the tree
                                        & beneath
                                        a rabbit's
                                        empty burrow.
                                        O listen
                                        can't You smell
                                        the howling Earth

its brutal mouth gaping   gasping   for the air   of You   the error of   hope.

FORTY-TWO DAYS UNTIL THE ELECTION—

Drowsy from inhaling the sharp September sun,
I nearly forget what is happening beyond my porch—
even as it persists like the hum of a low flying plane circling
over and over. Or the abundance of insects teasing the air.
Last night, I mistook a human call for an owl's.
Confused the international space station for a shooting star.
Recently I watched a mother bear and her cubs
pilfer a trash can before catching my scent, scurrying off.
My sister says *It is hard work, being human.*
But I think humans are hard work for the bears
and the migrating birds dodging our empty office towers.
When a flag-flying pickup rumbles past,
I realize I've been holding my breath again.

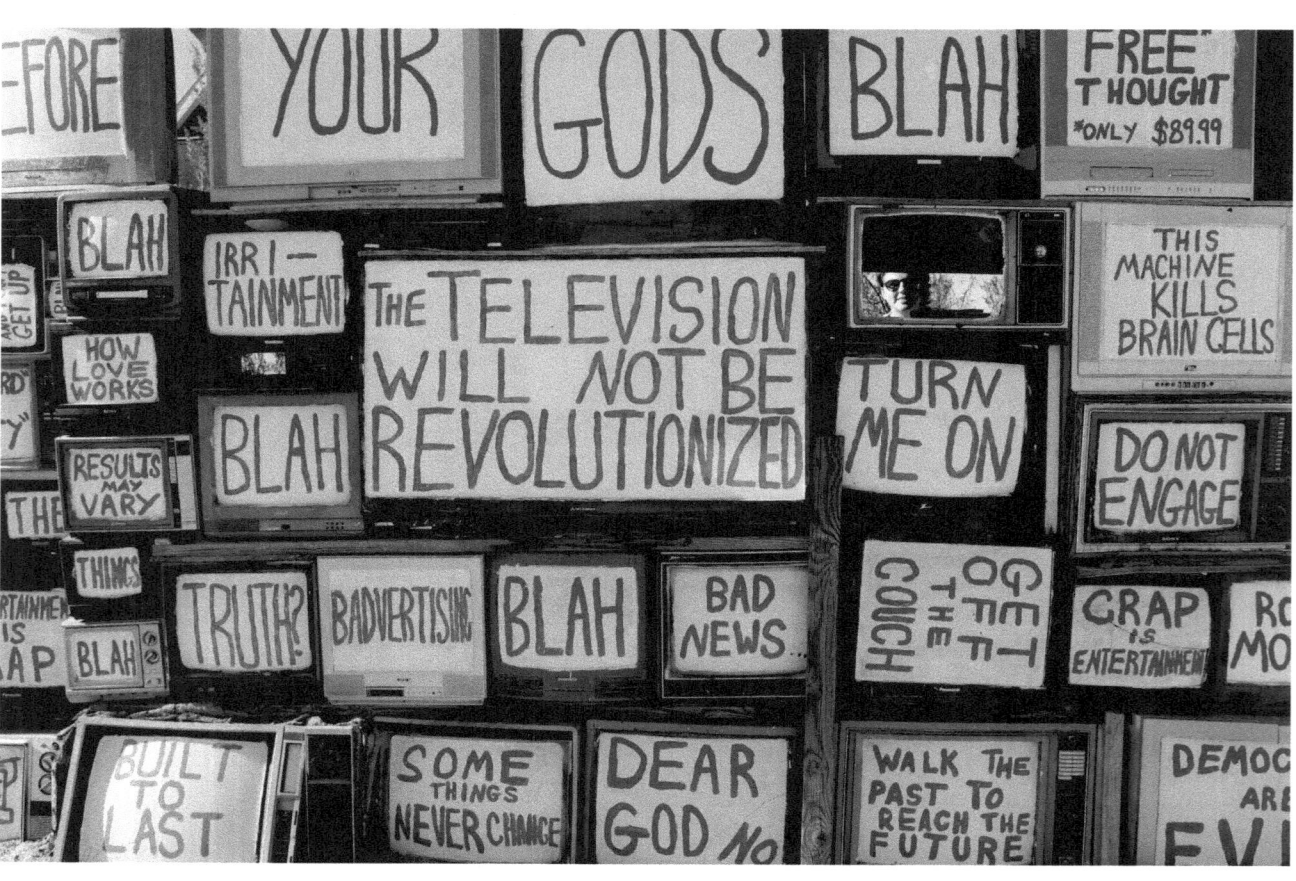

FISHING

With fingertips, I peel off the skin, then debone soft salmon flesh
the hue of autumn leaves, the late afternoon sky.

I recently read a poem about fishing, but it was really about desire,
failure and ultimately forgiveness, and it ended with *praise*.

A friend tattoos *seek joy* on her wrist.
Challenges me to write joy in this season of venison and bitter greens.

So, I imagine myself in the blue of Greece,
drinking Assyrtiko and picking Xiphias off the bone.

And then I become the fish, swimming down the gullet. If you desire
something for a long time when it arrives you feel relief,

and then grief. There have been five mass extinctions
in the life of planet Earth—the shark has survived four.

I keep thinking of the Bob Dylan line *he not busy being born
is busy dying* and wonder if *busy* is the issue here.

I've spent my life on the pages of a planner.
But now in the uncluttered space between days, I *hear the faint sound of oars*.

Then imagine Jonah in a fishing trawler wrestling Hokusai-size waves,
the kind that minnow a mountain, and God sends him into the belly of a whale.

I have drowned once and will again. Perhaps I've angered God.

Perhaps God is the shark in this story.

And survival is a dhow, is a mistral.
Yet—ah that quick tsk of hope—yet

the act of a tree shedding leaves is one of conservation. A gasp of exuberance,
before letting go like a salmon dying after spawning.

MISSIVE TO MY FATHER FROM THE NOW

And you will wonder where the salmon have gone.
And I will respond about the physics of water
and the artistry of land sculpture.
And doesn't that sound less damning
to your ears now?

And if you ask how I am, I will tell you—
some days, I watch the sea
as if it's my child, intent
on knowing her future. But how can I?

Even you father, who exists
beyond the temporal,
can look back to before ashes—
yours and the world's—how the light
glistened like fish scales every evening.
Such furious beauty and the promise of seasons
casting one perfect arc after another.

Then *one morning all that was burning.*

And not just the oil fields and cities.
And not just the woodlands and mountains.
And not just the meadows and vineyards.
And not just the suburbs.
And not just the lakes and rivers and streams.
And not just the seas.

There is a seething. I can't tell you how it began.
Exhumed. As if our skin had also burned, revealing
dark bones tethered in anger's muscle.
And I am frightened.

I would say I wish you were here, father—
but I left you sleeping.
And when we meet in my dreams,
I tell you of my home of seagulls and wind—
how I wake to their cries and worry,
of the rains that beat back the flames,
of the beloveds and language that sustain me.

EVEN AFTER ALL THESE YEARS

Each shift in motion begins with one bird's fear, a feather trigger.
Maybe it's a wind uptick or the startle of reflection in the Wadden Sea

that sets the starlings' murmuration. Millions, black in flight, in dance,
in Denmark. A form of madness, the starlings chattering in a single voice.

For love of Shakespeare, we speak starling, our mouths black with feathers.
I want to dance. But you refuse to lead. Isn't that a form of backstepping,

of creating space between us? In the wingspan of distance
from your body to mine, we could hold a lit candle or a child.

The European starlings arrived in crates as a gift of improvement
to the New World—a sonnet of birdsong released into Central Park.

Word travels with speed. So, when you tell me you still love me,
it wings past me. Say it again, louder. You know I'm a flight risk.

Once, we found each other before a congregation, vowing unison.
Last night, your body folded around mine. We slept like that as starlings

swept the night sky. *Stunning* you say, meaning the murmuration of birds—
improbable beauty on an otherwise ordinary day.

SPLIT SECOND

In the before
dawn's fuzzy
incoherent light
you say *listen*
you say you hear
a washing
machine I think
you hear my blood
washing
through my arteries
my heart filling
flushing
but okay I'll listen
& hear through
the open window
snails
nibbling
on young grape leaves
leaving a thin
trail of drying slime
& naked stems
sometimes
I hear the mouths
of moths
on my cashmere
sweaters
the weather of wing
dust falling
on sleeves
I take small stitches
to mend
the holes
sometimes

a spider casts off
its web to dangle
into the fragrant
air of our sleep
I listen
for humming
the song you hear
in the space
between
us the bristle
of your skin
pressing
against my nape
where I lodge
the fears
that queue around
the block of me
as if waiting for
a concert I often hear
their conversation
like an electric
toothbrush
or a horsefly
circling
until afternoon heat
slows each wing
beat
every fear
hovers for a split
second
before
leaving me
fanning sluggish air
pulling my hair
off my nape
sweat tracking

a thin streak of salt
a snail trail
maybe
in the shell I lug
it's the brain of me
thinking always
thinking of what (?)
thinking of what
to eat thinking
of espresso's whir
& shush
the soft whip of milk
an eggshell crack
such a brightness
in the pan
oh & avocado
slipping
from its skin
its pit
heavy like a kidney
an organ I rarely
consider
perhaps you hear
my kidneys churning
washing
my body's
laundry clean
of regrets—
the clothesline of white
sheets surrendering to
the next thought
in the dream
I just woke from
I was racing a brutal
storm
lightning striking

my bare
feet running
a trail of footprints
on fire
running to where (?)
then a cliff
before I woke
to you
holding me
steady wash
of breath
on my nape
& I felt your body
shift as it left
a cream
the way we leave
our home
unlocked
when we walk the dog
in the evening
& then I opened
my eyes
to the before
dawn's light
fuzzy incoherent
you saying *listen*
I hear a washing
machine I think
you hear
my blood
washing
through my arteries
my heart
filling.

TIME CAPSULE

Sleep Journal, 2024

Same dream: I stand cliff's edge in a storm.
Far below is a dark river. I must leap be-
yond the outcropping, boulder sprawl. I
don't know the river's depth or where it
leads. As I dive, a feather of blue sky—

PERHAPS THIS IS A PRAYER

When my eye holds the iridescent
        wing of a kingfisher for the split
                second it soars over the river Avon,

I feel the presence
        of a god. One that sprays
                the reeds with butterflies, feeds

wheat seeds to the most common
        sparrow. When my friend bends to tame
                the wildness of flower beds brimming

with dahlias and mutters about the mole,
        I say that is the god I'm talking about—the one
                who invites us to tunnel into the hungry earth.

Over a lunch harvested from the garden,
        we debate the existence of heaven and hell.
                Knowing only the temporal—

how the river twists its body to embrace the land,
        and longing silvers the heaving willow.
                So, when I say I imagine there is a god,

it's because from this morning's open window,
        I inhaled honeysuckle and jasmine. Heard
                god in the syncopation of birdsong.

Faith found this follower at my most tedious self—
        cornered in a cul-de-sac, the summer's heat beating
                like an old heart. Me, kneed by the burden

of body. A body now tilting
        into a breeze gathering upward.

IV.

Autumn

I have allowed the quarrel
of moving birds to comfort me.
        —Kwame Dawes

There was no weeping, just feathers passing.
And I am here now listening for day
        —Jorie Graham

TAKE FIVE

The tempo changes. Rain in late August.
Wildfire season extinguished.

As my email clutters with democratic emergencies, I play
Brubeck's *Take Five* on loop like when I was seventeen
driving through green, green, green. Untarnished by sunlight.

Listen to the drum solo. An enjambment.
Off-kilter. Giddy. Like love.
Yes, let's say its love.
Such an unstable, impromptu gesture.
The rhythm hesitating—

a syncopation, teetering.
I plant a yard sign, phone bank, donate the small change
of eighth notes. Each beat,

a brightening. Again, the brush over drum,
shuffle, shuffle over cymbal.

I'm vowing to stay alive with the man I love—
as the horn sheds its clothing on the floor.

NOTES

"I pray for time/to deal with now. no, I pray to Time" is from Danez Smith's poem "relativity" from *Bluff*. Copyright © 2024 by Danez Smith. Reprinted by permission of the poet and Graywolf Press, Minneapolis, Minnesota.

I. Winter

"We are living through a time/that needs to be lived through us" is from Adrienne Rich's poem "The Will to Change" (*Adrienne Rich 1950–2012*, W.W. Norton, 2018).

"Adieu, farewell, earth's bliss;/This world uncertain is;" is from "A Litany in Time of Plague" written in 1593 by Thomas Nashe (1567–1601).

"Accidie"
The poem takes its title from the medieval Latin *accidia*, descendant from the Greek *acedia*. In this usage, it conveys spiritual sloth (once considered the eighth deadly sin).

"Continuum"
"this residence of woe." is a partial line from Dante Alighieri's *Inferno*, Canto V. The full sentence is "O thou! who to this residence of woe/Approachest?" (Henry Francis Cary translation, 1814).

1 January 2020
"Auld lang syne" is a traditional song sung to bid farewell to the old year at the stroke of midnight on New Year's Eve. It is based on a poem by Robert Burns written in 1788 after an old Scottish folksong.

Winter/Spring 2020
"Wo warst du wann?" German tr: "Where were you when?"
"À votre santé" French tr: "To your health!"

In Shinto, deceased women are traditionally dressed in white kimonos. When a white kimono fastens left over right it is a sign of death.

Yuki onna (Japanese tr: "Snow woman") is a mythic Japanese folklore character who preys on travelers in the winter mountains. The legend tells that the yuki onna will often fall in love with their intended prey.

One of the Major Arcana cards of the tarot is the 'death' card. It depicts the Skeleton Reaper and features a skeleton riding a white horse.

"I had not thought death had undone so many" is a line from 'Burial of the Dead' section in T.S. Eliot's *The Waste Land* (Harcourt, Brace & World, Inc., 1962).

"Following the river of death downstream" is a lyric from Art Garfunkel's "Bright Eyes." "Bright Eyes" was written by Mike Batt and performed by Art Garfunkel on the soundtrack of the 1978 animated film *Watership Down*. The song also appears on Garfunkel's albums *Fate for Breakfast* (U.K. 1979) and *Scissors Cut* (U.S. 1981).

"Che ci toglie il respire" (Italian tr: "You take my breath away"). It's a lyric from "Grazie Roma" by Antonello Venditti. During the pandemic lockdown, Italians sung "Grazie Roma" from their balconies.

Winter 2020-21

"L'Inverno allegro non molto" references the first movement of the "Winter" violin concerti by Italian composer Antonio Vivaldi. Between 1718-1720 Vivaldi composed four concertis which became the *"Le quattro Stagioni"* or "Four Seasons".

The images *"barbarous king"* and *"a burnished throne"* are from the "A Game of Chess" section in T.S. Eliot's *The Waste Land*, Harcourt, Brace & World, Inc., 1962.

"Bring me flesh and bring me wine. Bring me pine logs hither " is a lyric from "Good King Wenceslas" written by John Mason Neale and Thomas Helmore in 1853 and has become a Christmas caroling staple.

"Yes, something's wrong. That restless" is a lyric from James Taylor's "Something's Wrong" which appeared as a track on his debut album *James Taylor*, 1968, Apple Records.

"Darkness and devils! Saddle my horses, call my train together!" is a line from Shakespeare's *King Lear*, Act 1, scene 4. (*The Riverside Shakespeare*, Houghton Mifflin Co., 1974).

"to run, stamping one's feet at each moment" is translated from Antonio Vivaldi's *"L'Inverno"* sonnet (part of the *"Le Quattro Stagioni"* sonnets which were published along with his violin concerti of the same title) in 1725.

"Do you remember/Nothing?" are lines from "A Game of Chess" section in T.S. Eliot's *The Waste Land,* (Harcourt, Brace & World, Inc., 1962).

The King of Spades symbolizes a predator, a man of bad faith, who seeks to use others for his own ends in cartomancy and tarot.

Winter 2022

"Who could forget the buttercup poet on the Capital steps" alludes to Amanda Gorman who served as the inaugural poet at the inauguration of President Biden, January 20, 2021. She wore a yellow coat by the designer Prada.

"Let's go backwards when forward fails" is a lyric from "Everything Old is New Again". Written by Peter Allen and Carole Bayer Sager. Performed by Peter Allen on the soundtrack (A&M Records) for the film *All That Jazz,* 1979.

цей світ (tsey svit) is Ukrainian for "this world".

"Some will say none of this never happened…we were/happy and went to see the puppet shows in the park" is from the poem "And Yet, on Some Nights" by Ilya Kaminsky from *Deaf Republic* (Graywolf Books, 2019).

Summer/Fall 2022

"Good night Bess!/Good night Lulu! Good night Mabel!" echos the lines "Good night, ladies; good night, sweet ladies; good night, good night" in "A Game of Chess" section from T.S. Eliot's *The Waste Land* (Harcourt, Brace & World, Inc., 1962).

"*¿Dónde está?*" Spanish tr. "Where is…".

Francis Bacon was an Irish painter (1909-1992) who was known for his "grotesque imagery—contorted limbs, howling mouths agape, blood" (*artnet*). The Centre Pompidou held a Francis Bacon exposition in 2019-20.

"minds full of fluff" is a nodding reference to A.A. Milne's *Winnie-the-Pooh* (Methuen, 1926).

"as if/my mind and body isn't my own" from Evie Shockley's poem "topsy talks about her role" in *semiautomatic* (Wesleyan University Press, 2017).

7 October 2023

"the past is rotting in the future—" is a line from Anna Akhmatova's "Poem without a Hero" (translated by D.M. Thomas, Akhmatova, Swallow Press, 1976).

Spring 2024—

"Something's always wrong. Again. Again. Again." is a lyric from Toad the Wet Sprocket's "Something's Always Wrong" from the album *Dulcinea*, 1994.

"Lasciate ogne speranza, voi ch'intrate" appears as the inscription over the Gates of Hell translating as "Abandon all hope, ye who enter here" in Dante Alighieri's *Inferno*, Canto III (Henry Francis Cary translation, 1814).

"Berieitstehen!" German tr. "Stand by".

"Then put your seatbelt on. Buckle up. Buckle up. Buckle up" are lyrics from Pearl Jam's "Buckle Up" on the *Gigaton* album released in 2020.

"Your time will come" is the refrain from Iron Maiden's "The Wicker Man" on the *Brave New World* album released in 2000 by EMI Records.

"Do you remember/Nothing?" are lines from "A Game of Chess" section in T.S. Eliot's *The Waste Land*, (Harcourt, Brace & World, Inc., 1962).

"Where are we now?/The moment you know/You know, you know" are lyrics from David Bowie's "Where Are We Now" that was recorded in secret after 9/11 at the Magic Shop in New York City. It was released as the lead single on the album *The Next Day*, 2013 by RCA Records.

II. Spring

"Time collapses between the lips of strangers" is from Audre Lorde's poem "Never to Dream of Spiders" (*The Collected Poems of Audre Lorde*, W.W. Norton, 1997). Reprinted by permission from W.W. Norton.

"Here from this century can you say/was it wild to be born?/Was there anything else like this, anything at all?" is from Brenda Hillman's poem "1951" which appeared in *poet.org's Poem-a-Day*. Reprinted with the poet's permission.

"In Search of Eden at the New York Botanical Garden"

The poem references the work and 2021 exhibition of the artist Yayoi Kusama at the New York Botanical Garden.

The poet Mark Doty read a draft poem at the Bryant Park Poetry series in July 2021 which included the line, *"no time/then but a single day"*.

III. Summer

"I do not know which god sent me,/To fall into the river/And fall in the fire." is from the poem "At the Gates" by Kofi Awoonor (*The Promise of Hope: New and Selected Poems 1964-2013*, University of Nebraska Press, 2014). Reprinted with permission from University of Nebraska Press.

"I know you are reading this poem, torn/between bitterness and hope." is from the section "XIII (Dedications)" in Adrienne Rich's poem "An Atlas of the Difficult World" (*Adrienne Rich 1950-2012*, W.W. Norton, 2018). Reprinted by permission from W.W Norton.

"On the Continuum"

The poem includes the line *"this is the way that faith asserts itself"* from Kwame Dawes poem "Shook Foil" (*Shook Foil, a Collection of Reggae Poems*, Peepal Tree Press, 1997).

The line *"e de mosche, e mosconi il Stuol furioso!"* is from Antonio Vivaldi's "L'Estate" sonnet (part of the *"Le Quattro Stagioni"* sonnets which were published in 1725 along with his violin concerti of the same title). It translates from the original Italian as "And by furious swarms of flies and hornets" in English.

"Lookout"

"Lookout" is a single poem in four sections that is in conversation with T.S. Eliot's *Four Quartets* (Faber and Faber, 1944). Each section of "Lookout" includes lines from the *Four Quartets*. Specifically,

Skagit Valley
> includes the following lines from the section 'Little Gidding':
> *"And what you thought you came for/is only a shell, a husk of meaning"* *"watching whence the smoke arose"* *"ash on an old man's sleeve"* and *"You came to kneel"*.

Into the Garden
> includes the following lines from the section 'Burnt Norton':
> *"Caught in the form of limitation"* and *"not here the darkness in this twittering world?"*.

Puget Sound
> includes the following lines from the section 'The Dry Salvages':
> *"the sea is all about us"* and *"the tolling bell"* and *"You came to kneel"* from 'Little Gidding'.

Feverish
> includes the following lines from the section 'East Coker':
> *"late roses filled with early snow"* *"another day/prepares for heat and silence"* *"and creatures of the summer heat"* and *"that destructive fire?"*

The poet referred to in 'Skagit Valley' and 'Into the Garden' is Jorie Graham and is based on Graham's conversation with David Naimon on the August 9, 2023, episode of his podcast "Between the Covers".

The "another poet" referred to in "Into the Garden" is Arthur Sze who was interviewed by David Naimon for the June 6, 2021 episode of the podcast "Between the Covers." During that conversation, Sze discussed scale in Chinese painting and relationality of the "I" that inspired the line "In Chinese paintings, humans appear as mites in a natural landscape—/the "I uncentered."

A Compendium of Collective Nouns referred to in 'Puget Sound' is by Mark Faulkner, Eduardo Lima Filho, Harriet Logan and Miraphora Mina of Woop Studios, (Chronicle Books, 2013).

"~~Un~~ending"

The poem's form was inspired by the poems in Jorie Graham's *Sea Change* (Ecco, 2008).

"Fishing"

The poem referenced in the second couplet is James Davis May's poem "Fishing Again at Thirty-Five" (*Unusually Grand Ideas*, Louisiana State University Press, 2023).

Bob Dylan's lyric *"he not busy being born is busy dying"* is from the song "It's Alright, Ma (I'm Only Bleeding)" which appeared originally on the album *Bringing It All Back Home,* released in 1965 by Columbia Records.

The poem includes the line "*hear the faint sound of oars*" from Jack Gilbert's "A Brief for the Defense" (*Collected Poems* by Jack Gilbert, Alfred A Knopf, 2012).

Hokusai was a Japanese ukiyou-artist (1760-1849) who was known for wood block prints including the famous "Great Wave" which depicts a fishing trawler encountering a tsunami. The Seattle Art Museum exhibited 200 of Hokusai's surviving artworks, 2023-24.

"Missive to My Father from the Now"

The poem incorporates the line "*one morning all that was burning*" and was inspired by Pablo Neruda's "*Explico Algunas Cosas*" as translated by Nathaniel Tarn (*Pablo Neruda Selected Poems: A Bilingual Edition*, Gardners Books, 1992).

"Even Now, After All These Years"

Was inspired by the photographer Soren Solkaer's exhibition *Black Sun* at the National Nordic Museum, 2023-24 which included the film *Black Sun* and was drawn from the book *Black Sun* (Edition Circle, 2023).

The poem references the importation and release into New York City's Central Park of 60 pairs of starlings in 1890 by Eugene Schieffelin who undertook to introduce the birds mentioned in Shakespeare's works into North America.

IV. Autumn

"*I have allowed the quarrel/of moving birds to comfort me.*" is from the Kwame Dawes poem "A Prayer to Light" (*Yale Review*, Fall 2024). Reprinted with permission from the poet.

"*There was no weeping, just feathers passing./And I am here now listening for day*" is from Jorie Graham's poem "Day" in the collection, *To 2040* (Copper Canyon Press, 2023). Reprinted with permission from the poet and Copper Canyon Press.

"Take Five"

"Take Five" was composed by Paul Desmond and first recorded in 1959 by the Dave Brubeck Quartet, appearing on their album *Time Out* (Columbia Records). "Take Five" is composed in the unorthodox quintuple meter. It is the top-selling jazz song of all time.

ACKNOWLEDGMENTS

Deep gratitude to the editors of these literary journals, anthologies and institutions for their recognition and publication of the following poems, sometimes in earlier versions. Thank you for believing in this work:

"Accidie" was published in *The Cortland Review*.

"Continuum" was published by *Terrain.org*.

"Even After All These Years" won *The Missouri Review's Jeffrey E. Smith Editors Prize for Poetry, 2022* and was published in *The Missouri Review*. It appears in the anthology of *Best Spiritual Literature Vol. 9* (Edited by Luke Hankins, Orison Press 2024).

"Fish Story" was published in *Bracken* and was nominated for a Pushcart Prize.

"Fishing" was published in *The Pinch Journal*.

"Forty-Two Days until the Election—" appeared in *Poets Reading the News*.

"In Search of Eden with Kasama at the New York Botanical Garden" appeared in *On the Seawall*.

"Lookout" was published in *One*. It received a Best of Net 2024 nomination.

"Perhaps This is a Prayer" won *The Missouri Review's Jeffrey E. Smith Editors Prize for Poetry, 2022* and was published in *The Missouri Review*. It was nominated for the Orison Press' *Best Spiritual Literature* in 2023.

"Split Second" appeared in *The Marrow* and is anthologized in *The Madrona Project: This Machine Is Made for Earth* (Edited by Michael Daley from Empty Bowl Press 2024).

"Time Capsule: Tax Return, 1958" and "Time Capsule: Ultrasounds, 1988, 1990, 1994" were published in *Couplet Poetry*.

"Time Capsule: Eye Mask, 2019" "Time Capsule: Diploma, 1980" "Time Capsule: Face Mask, 2020" "Time Capsule: Used Lube Tube, 2009-" were finalists for the Laurence Goldstein Poetry Prize (*Michigan Quarterly Review*).

Time Capsule: Photo with My Sisters, 1967" "Time Capsule: Class photo, 1969" "Time Capsule: Map of United States, 1973" "Time Capsule: Diploma, 1980" "Time Capsule: Company Retreat, 1986" "Time Capsule: Stiletto, 1986" "Time Capsule: Empty Pack of Marlboro Reds, 1988" "Time Capsule: Wooden Blocks, 1990-2002" "Time Capsule: Wall Street Journal, 2001" "Time Capsule: Water Bottle, 2006—" "Time Capsule: Used Lube Tube, 2009" and "Time Capsule: Family Wedding Photo, 2023" were published in *Blood Tree Literature*.

"Unending" appeared in *Image Journal*.

Thank you to the following artists whose beautiful work graces *tic tic tic*: Keith Skelton, Ester Moliné, Sutishi, Feri Ferdinan, Montes-Bradley, Utopia_88, Maggie Henfield, and James Crombie. And to Eric Falk for the stunning cover photograph "Passing Through Time" and Kelsey Chance for my swell author photograph. Special recognition to Jack Sinclair for his gorgeous photography throughout.

At the heart of *tic tic tic* is time—the era we are living through, history's expanse, and the seasons of our lives. But it wouldn't have been written or published without the extraordinary gift of time given by so many.

To the many teachers who have guided both my reading and writing of poetry, giving me the knowledge to write *tic tic tic*. And to the many literary lights who informed this work.

Enduring gratitude for the time devoted to the making of these poems by the poets in my writing workshops: Suzanne Edison, Donna Spruijt-Metz, Veronica Golos, Will Barnes, Martha Silano, Jed Myers, Tina Schulmann, Jill McCabe Johnson, Deborah Bacharach, Carolyne Wright, Ann Spiers, Robert McNamara, Cass Garison, Susan Landgraf, Sigrun Susan Lane, Dia Calhoun, Michele Bombardier, Cindy Veach, and Lillo Way. I am so fortunate to have your wisdom and friendship.

Huge thanks to my dear colleagues at *The Adroit Journal*, Peter LaBerge, Chris Crowder, Elaina Friedman, Kalpana Negi, David Roderick, and the entire staff who volunteer your time to make *The Adroit Journal* happen. It's amazing to be in the midst of so much talent. You lift me up!

Immense gratitude to the esteemed poets Major Jackson, Arthur Sze, Gabrielle Bates, and Diana Khoi Nguyen for your time spent with *tic tic tic* and the extraordinary gift of praise.

What a stroke of luck to have Cornerstone Press as the publisher for *tic tic tic*. Beginning with Dr. Ross K. Tangedal for your enthusiasm for this book, concept to include art, and sharp editorial presence. Excellent editing by Paige Biever, and to Allison Lange, Sam Bjork, and Sophie McPherson for guiding this book through design, production, and into the world. I also want to thank Heather Brown of Mind the Bird Media for publicity, and Scott Miller and Nicky Sinclair for designing this powerful cover.

I'm forever grateful that my mother read poetry to my sisters, brother, and me, and that you continue to show up in so many ways to support my writing. You are my inspiration. As is the family that I've created, Jack, Hallie, and Nicky and their loves, Jenna, Makaela, and Leda, and for my granddaughter Audrey. This book is for you and your generations. Finally, I couldn't write without the incredible love and support of my husband, Scott.

Above all, thank you dear reader. In these chaotic times, I am grateful to all who bring light.

Heidi Seaborn is the author of *Marilyn: Essays & Poems* (Collector's Edition of *An Insomniac's Slumber Party with Marilyn Monroe*) (2022) and *Give a Girl Chaos {see what she can do}* (2019). Her poems and essays have appeared in *AGNI, Beloit Poetry Journal, Blackbird, Brevity, Copper Nickel, The Cortland Review, Image, Financial Times of London, LitHub, The Mississippi Review, ONE, Pedestal, The Penn Review, Pleiades, Plume, Poetry Northwest, Rattle, SWWIM*, Terrain.org, and *The Slowdown*, in several anthologies, as a film, in a political pamphlet, *Body Politic* (2017), and in three chapbooks: *Finding My Way Home* (2018), and *BITE MARKS* (winner of the 2020 *Comstock Review* Chapbook Prize, 2021) and *Once a Diva* (2021).

She is the winner of *The Missouri Review*'s Jeffrey E. Smith Editor's Prize and has won or been shortlisted for over sixty literary awards or recognitions. She currently serves as executive editor of *The Adroit Journal*. She holds a B.A. from Stanford University and a M.F.A. in Poetry from New York University. She lives in Seattle. Her work can be found at heidiseabornpoet.com

www.ingramcontent.com/pod-product-compliance
Lightning Source LLC
Chambersburg PA
CBHW041144120626
46547CB00020B/3106

9781968148072